VEXATIONS

PHOENIX POETS

Edited by Srikanth Reddy

Vexations

ANNELYSE GELMAN

THE UNIVERSITY OF CHICAGO PRESS
CHICAGO & LONDON

The University of Chicago Press, Chicago 60637
The University of Chicago Press, Ltd., London

For more information, contact the University of Chicago Press, 1427 E. 60th St., Chicago, IL 60637.
Published 2023
Printed in the United States of America

32 31 30 29 28 27 26 25 24 23 2 3 4 5

ISBN-13: 978-0-226-82611-0 (paper)
ISBN-13: 978-0-226-82612-7 (e-book)
DOI: https://doi.org/10.7208/chicago/9780226826127.001.0001

Library of Congress Cataloging-in-Publication Data

Names: Gelman, Annelyse, author.
Title: Vexations / Annelyse Gelman.
Other titles: Phoenix poets.
Description: Chicago : The University of Chicago Press, 2023. | Series: Phoenix poets
Identifiers: LCCN 2022040906 (print) | ISBN 9780226826110 (paperback) | ISBN 9780226826127 (ebook)
Subjects: LCGFT: Poetry.
Classification: LCC PS3607.E463 V39 2023 (print) | DCC 811/.6–dc23/eng/20220920
LC record available at https://lccn.loc.gov/2022040906

♾ This paper meets the requirements of ANSI/NISO Z39.48-1992 (Permanence of Paper).

VEXATIONS

Even the grass was coming up positive
Soles beading little match tips of blood
A reticular glitch made me saccade like crazy
Clouds like anemones, electric fortresses
A dandelion fluff might fly in your mouth
As you ate a hamburger, the last hamburger

That was the year the hurricanes began
I hardly swelled but felt her features forming
There were airs, waters, places, daughters
I pressed my eyes dry like flowers-in-book
A tree couldn't move without tearing its roots
There was no other world to bring a child into

Crowds coagulated to watch falling bodies
Daughter depicted them on my uterine walls
We were firm believers in teleology, at first
Night crews came like sexton beetles
Men with bird masks and wheelbarrows
After a while there were too many to clean up

Just the ginkgos, a parent might say, regarding the smell
Sometimes a crater held the imprint of a face
The dominant metaphor for the brain was the computer
Subterranean romance, romance of alterity
Who notices the horse becomes the horse, went the saying
I was terrified, of course, I had noticed the mane

I lay down in the flower bed, fresh in the dirt
She pushed out of me, they cut her in cold water
From a rubber hose, red daughter, red birth
The timbre of an infant's cry foreshadowed its destiny
If there is no pain, you may not be injured, went the saying
Or you may have severed the nerve

It was around that time I started taking the pills
The jingle went, *Elsewhere, Elsewhere,* that was the only lyric
They made my skin glossy like it was about to cry
The body became basically a repository of data
A craving was fungible, you could want pretty much anything
A body was fungible, you could be pretty much anyone

Moths, lots, swarmed the lighthouse lamps
Ships crashed into cliffs, one after another, elements emerged
Between our legs like coiled appendages of jellyfish
It was around that time I started taking the pills
Cultivars rolled out each season like new hemlines
I carried the procedures within me, dormant like viruses

The environment updated itself at regular intervals
Sometimes a new species of tree frog, sometimes a lethal infection
People played chess across unfathomable expanses
Studies said fetuses preferred wasps to orchids
Exquisitely dependent, a scientist might say, regarding a spiderweb
We lost everything, a clown might say, regarding the quake

A person might pay thousands to utter the word *dapple*
Thousands more to say *dapple* in front of another person
We crawled out of the seas and smuggled their salts
Inside each of our cells, each of our portable oceans
Everyone was a labor theorist, no one was a laborer
It was quaint—crass, even—to disturb the air with sound waves

Creamy like a library, someone wrote, regarding madness
Creamy, like certain roses, regarding a woman's cheeks
Creamy bursts, regarding flares dropped from choppers
Creamy, a prayer between two flights
Creamy, the inner surface of one thigh
We didn't know what to do with our garbage

Situations were generally regarded with suspicion
Every extinction was a planned obsolescence
Wretched, a professor might say, regarding the culture
It was forbidden to cause a *situation* to occur
As for commodities, half the toothpaste was poison
Man-made lakes and their too-accurate colors

A bark beetle inscribed an elm illegibly
Opaque bodies transparentized where they touched
Soft pop of grubs disclosing their imperiled parts
A tender-tongued admirer espied an especially attractive
Shrub with which to munch away the afternoon
Sometimes we felt sick from eating too much food

Imagining the future was one wholesome hobby
If you couldn't imagine you could just go by rote, it was impossible
To tell the difference, a person's eyes didn't really unfocus
When they had a picture in their mind, not like in the novels
Besides, we were not communicating so much
As auditioning sentences for each other

With devout fervor we humiliated one another
A person might pay thousands to be made chaste again
Celebrate, a counselor might say, regarding productivity
People lay in alcoves with their faces to the concrete
In the overgrown parking lot of a reputation laundering firm
The jingle went, *Elsewhere, Elsewhere,* I sang it in my sleep

In front of the police chief's house a live oak
Cracked the sidewalk like crème brûlée
Beneath the paving stones there was not a beach
There were only life-sustaining elements
We would move through life quickly and never get hurt
Like a hand brushed through a lit wick, unburnt

Once a month they took down the missing person posters
Pornography of streetlamps stripped even of staples
It was difficult back then to articulate a thought
Meaning a negligee for words to slip out of
Denuded like a peeled apple, a *situation*
It's difficult now to explain how difficult it was

An elevator door might cut off an interrupting arm
Flopped there on the linoleum like a dying carp
Colony collapse, a lover might say
Your last lover, enthusiastically rimming your earhole
We felt we were at the beginning of something
We already essentially felt we were already essentially doomed

I pet her behind the ears like a little rabbit
She looked at a word until she could read it
Daughter crawled under the credenza after the dog
The pair of them sniffing out something I couldn't share in
Burrowed in blankets at the bottom of the bed
Her shoulder blades warm against my feet

A human heart might spontaneously dissect
Or hoard your blood in its dark bunker
Nurses tested the wounded for the apology reflex
The reservoir gave up its annual protest
In the town square painters tore out the mane with their teeth
Citizens stood by to learn the song of the crying horse

It was around that time I started taking the pills
The jingle went, *Elsewhere, Elsewhere,* I sang it in my bathrobe
Touching a serrated edge to a substantial loaf
Colorful smoke rose from the mouth of an Erlenmeyer flask
Daughter in the school play, hoisted to the ceiling
To move the angel, they tied a rope around its neck

I went to a bright mall with a fire in its center
The ceiling was made of thick glass, magnifying glass
Concentrating sunlight into the center of the fire
Over the PA someone announced a sale on underwear
Photons were bouncing off my face, lost forever
Precarity made me swoon, perfectly breathtaking

Over the PA someone recited a list of integers
The meaning of which was not intelligible to me
25, 84, 41, 81, I fell absolutely in love with the voice, my *Elsewhere*
I felt sure that if the numbers concluded, I would die
The mall twinkled with a promising aura of possibility
The voice stopped and I did not die, ergo I was not in love

We purchased equipment for sleeping safely outdoors
We stored this equipment carefully until it was garbage
Newscasters invented new verbs to accommodate the news
Over the PA someone announced that the mall was closing
People came up to me and said, *Did you hear?*
People came up to me and said, *What mall?*

Sitting in silence aroused the neighbors
Minute exchanges of power were a universal currency
An incarcerated man asked for a photograph of the sun
I found the eggs and set a trap in the pantry
We were cloven, we equipped ourselves with debt
We wrote contracts with the rivers and signed them

The word *impending* no longer prefaced *collapse*
The earth smelled like shit from runoff and rainlessness
Like my predecessors, I suffered from a crisis of attention
Speculate meant *to imagine* but also *to gamble*
We were hopeless with risk, helpless, rapt
I put the oval on the back of my tongue

Colonies popped out of empire like mushrooms
Coral reefs thinned out their amenities, the entire pluck
Could be removed en masse for complete evaluation
Daughter landed wrong at the bottom of a slide
The weight of the ice melt slowly tilted the Earth
As for the starry crown, we didn't know what to do with it

We volunteered to make phone calls to lonely people
A shy mimosa cringed when you touched it
A compound connected with a receptor and a smell occurred
Daughter stared at her plate, she wouldn't eat
Until I told her exactly how much yellow the yolk contained
In the rainforest each animal occupied its verticality

I got an occurrence for talking wrong to a stranger
I distracted daughter while they arrested my neighbor
A man got put on chain and transferred south
A mother taught her daughter where to put her mouth
Beginners in a language all learned the same phrases
You could still drink straight from the ground in places

It was around that time I was accused of faking it
There was text everywhere, lush, orchestral text
A procession of violent images culminating in a fact
Like my predecessors, I suffered from a crisis of authenticity
Elsewhere, Elsewhere, I would have defended it with my life
Reaching for comfort like a leaf toward light

Your song is a privilege, not a right, went the saying
Who sings least lovely in the field shall have it revoked
Head of horse waving in wind, positively fluttering
We pledged allegiance to the last fascist whinny
Still, we gnawed the sweetest bits of all the sweetest trees
Ashes in the atmosphere made sunsets last for weeks

One day daughter sliced her palm open on the gate
In the backyard where the possum wouldn't stop
Hissing, we hit it with a hockey stick but it wouldn't budge
Its tail was thick and pale, like the forearm of a man
We punish by putting him in a cell where he can't empathize
With anyone, we hit him with a hockey stick, but he won't budge

I jiggled the faucet and out sputtered the muck
The cut was wide but not deep, praise be
A toy train passed behind a toy mountain and disappeared
Have you ever watched a child develop solitude?
Doubt comes over her like a sleeper wave on a gorgeous day . . .
The blood was common-poppy red, the grass chroma-key green

Waves of action potentials crashed into my brain
Daughter flinched when I daubed the necessary stuff
Beneath our feet the whole entire world passed
Bit by bit through the bodies of the earthworms
—*Mama,* she said, as I wrapped her bandage
—*Do you feel how much it hurts?*

I had the feeling I should start collecting something
I had the feeling toxins were accumulating in my body
I had the feeling my personal history was indistinguishable from toxicity
Smog spawned dark murmurations over suburbs
Events slid into each other, marvelously promiscuous
Pronouns sludged through me, entirely inadequate

Sometimes daughter tried to write with my hand
A subdivided insect ate one bite of each available plant
With its diffuse body, spreading like an oil spill
Over the roses, a seed dispersed by exploding
And the mountains rose, purpled to the hilt
All of a sudden is how fish occupied the land

People went over waterfalls in wooden barrels
People built a road straight through the base
Of the oldest living tree in the world
The specialist took a core sample
From daughter's spine with a fat needle
Everything she'd ever felt was there, preserved in layers

The economy of attention was an economy of care
People marked their children's heights on doorframes
People had a picnic on a lovely day
The question of etiology was a question of blame
Daughter held a frog in her hand, enjoying her interaction
The specialist frowned as I answered the questions

Have you ever watched a child develop terror?
Narrative comes over her like the violet hour at the end of an endless evening . . .
It was hard to forget new information, even if you learned it was false
You had to remember the information *and* that it was false
It was like walking up a tempered-glass staircase into a cloud
From which there was no wisdom one could carry down

An anthropologist held a baby and the baby neighed
After you died they reset the sensor and put it in someone else
There were droughts, floods, heat waves, plagues
Acts of God, sending thoughts, nonbreaking space
Probability choreographed our collective movements
There were no fire drills, there were only fires

Especially fires, enough fires to keep us in practice
You should have seen it, our balletic forfeiture of possessions
An almost virtuosic mastery of mass evacuations
Daughter dreaming with her face toward the crowds
Turned slowly in her sleep like night-blooming datura
Searchlight-through-curtains, moon-through-clouds

At dawn the bugs died down and the birds started up
The dog stared at a photograph of a forest like it was a window
Willows along the canal were smothered in something cotton candy–esque
A dense tangle of orbs and cobs and sheets
Beings decomposed and became other beings
At dusk the bugs started up and the birds died down

Creamy pudding, someone wrote, regarding knowledge
Mown clover augmented redundant smells
People in movies confused her, they always had something to say
A figure's hand was still encased in the marble block
A scheme always failed if you watched it being hatched
The formula made drama a foregone conclusion

The specialist put sharp metal into daughter's arm
The specialist put soft plastic down her throat
The specialist put piezoelectric crystals onto her wrists
The specialist put her head in a sound like a propeller
Falling out of the sky and into a municipal swimming pool
Not otherwise specified, said the specialist

A person wearing gloves kept saying *attachment*
Porous daughter, who couldn't domesticate her noticing
They would take her from me and put her in a home
She would lie on ironed sheets until she had no personality
Like that woman who couldn't pour a cup of tea
Because it was *frozen, like a glacier*

The dominant metaphor for the body was the engine
The dominant metaphor for the city was the body
The dominant metaphor for identity was consumption
Sometimes a brain got too big, holes had to be drilled
To make room, I committed the first page of the economics textbook to memory
People always want more, no matter how much they have already

People rode gondolas to nice-looking viewpoints
People learned how to make concrete and then forgot
People saw ambulance lights through someone else's front door's stained glass
  paneling
People sat in the backs of taxis and professed intentions
In a fake Russian schoolhouse an intern sprinkled
Fake dust onto the fake wooden school desk

On the assembly line I assembled a single petiole
Plastids eroded my prints until I couldn't scan in
They severed me to propagate below the aerial root
A frond, flattered with a fingertip, unfurled
A cassette tape dissolved like a body in acid
We regretted our failure to explore the oceans

People built robots to clean the dust off solar panels
A mirrored array bounced sunbeams to a collection tower
Birds flew through the light and were cooked in midair
People built robots to pick up the bird corpses
The desert blew into the forest and civilized the trees
Over the PA someone said, *A diamond is forever!*

As for the wristband—just as, for the corn, it was cheaper
To throw it away than to sell it—it was cheaper
To buy a new watch than to fix it—just as, for the cancer
It was cheaper to throw you away than to treat it
When the robots broke, we piled them with old car parts behind chain-link fences
We didn't know what to do with our garbage

In a pocket of ordinary time I met a horse, he was two big warm lips under my lips
He looked at me the way people looked at each other in alleyways
Before the *situation*, trying to decide if they ought to be nervous
When I held bobby pins in my mouth braiding daughter's hair
And she cried when the fox said, *Please—tame me!*
And she cried when the boy said, *I want to, very much, but—*

The waiting room was painted pale green with big purple horrible flowers
There were real plants in plastic pots in the corner, there was a pamphlet with an unshucked ear on it, there was pink mold growing on the ceiling in moist stalactitic protuberances
There was a poster of a painting of a girl about daughter's age, standing in a snowy field
She had bare feet and a long white dress
In the folds of which squirmed, half-formed
Many very little white rabbits . . .

The waiting room smelled like the ball of cotton in a bottle of pills
A man with a rusty metal cart began watering the plants
There was something wrong with the many very little white rabbits . . . they melted into the dress . . . the rabbits emerged from it, merged with it, were it—
The man produced a pair of shears and bent
To prune a leaf browning at the edges
On the ceiling pulsed the pink mold

The article called the tundra a *giant white layer cake*
Gazes were always *attaching to* things and *tearing away* again
A magpie pecked at the appropriate array
I tore my gaze away from the many very little white rabbits . . .
Daughter on the carpet, cradling the amputated leaf, reciting her litany
The emotions our subcortical brain networks engendered . . . various . . .

—*No, no, no, no, no,* said daughter
She was squeezing the meager green stump to stem
The flow of whatever it was she felt in there
Already words like *good* and *bad* had a lustrous appeal
Like glazed donuts, it was comforting to suppose
Something could be *good* or *bad,* for example

Consonance was good, which was *good*
Dissonance was bad, which was *bad*
—*It hurts,* said daughter
—*I think something's wrong,* said daughter
—*I think something's wrong with me,* said daughter
The days of disappearing into a throng were over

I lifted her from the floor, I slapped her in the face
I don't know what came over me, isn't that what people say?
Horses greeting each other touched noses
I glared at the doctors in a petrochemical haze
She was heavier than I remembered, but then
It had been how-long since I'd picked her up

After the attack the truck full of donated blood
Stopped for gas on the way to the hospital
Courage was a *situation,* I didn't want to be seduced
Studies said we should titrate the moonlight
Looking at money made me think in money
I extracted a resource from the milieu

The specialist said, *Persistent and indiscriminate receptivity*
We boiled in the sun beneath snowcapped mountains
We had a word for stepping on someone's face with a boot
We had a word for the least liked member of a group
Who would preserve the smell of an expired carton of milk?
Radical, a critic might say, regarding sincerity

A person setting their body on fire understood faith
The specialist said, *Encounter-Loss Therapy*
A tomato had a sticker saying what country it was from
The most popular pets were bred to thrive on submission
You could cut an animal open and put your body in its skin
If you got too warm, you could take it off again

Blissful, a survivor might say, regarding the aftermath
Young people were turning up in coat closets
With notes on their bedside tables saying sorry for the mess
We didn't know what to do with our garbage
We were afraid the world would dilute our interiority
But the world was our interiority

The box stridulated and daughter opened the lid
Inside was a single grasshopper, fluorescent green, legs rigid, five eyes
I could see her see the grasshopper see her, all at once
They killed the grasshopper, and she screamed, I watched her watch
Their eyes, all five, those suddenly emptied estates
In whose hallways she could no longer hear her own echo

A conspiracy of hoofprints circled each other in sawdust
I just wanted to feel something was what people said
When they stepped into acid rain and opened their mouths
They killed the grasshopper, and she screamed
They killed the grasshopper, and she screamed
Over the PA someone asked about a lost wallet

They killed the grasshopper, and she screamed
Creamy smoothness, someone wrote, regarding a fog-wreathed sea
A little nectar was enough to make two hummingbirds
Fight to the death, we found the loser's body beneath the feeder
An absolutely lovely postcoital aphasia used to come over me
The plant is the leaf, went the saying

I tried not to panic, it only made her panic
We begrudged our bodies their relentless neediness
Shoals of deviance darted around like fissile material
The form of the danger was an emanation of energy
As for the youngest, there were tender age facilities
We worshipped progress, there was nothing else to worship

They killed the grasshopper until she couldn't scream anymore
After the session her face was stained with screams
Pain is weakness leaving, went the saying
I buckled the seat belt and shifted into first, I could hear her
Forehead knocking against the window as we went over the bumps
Her breath smelled mealy, like old fruit

Driving in grids made me think in grids
I sent little pictures of hearts from the waiting room
We played piano for the dog and laughed when he sang
Children learned the word *and* and then the word *or*
Children lied when asked where they'd been
A child was both more and less of a person than an adult

I read her the book about the little rabbit
Who tells his mother he is running away
If you become a little boy and run into a house, said the mother bunny, I said
I will become your mother and catch you in my arms and hug you, I said
I read her the book about the little rabbit
Who says goodnight to every object in the room

People turned blue in Jacuzzis full of ice cubes
People posing for portraits playacted tolerance
They killed the grasshopper, and she screamed
Daughter reclined on a chaise longue with a lute rendered in perspective
And lifted her elbows to expose her abilities
Over the PA someone breathed quickly in and out

It was around that time I started taking the pills
The jingle went, *Elsewhere, Elsewhere,* I mouthed it in my sundress
They made my eyes glisten like coated-with-dew
They killed the grasshopper, and she screamed
Elsewhere, her hands stained with their green
Blood, her hands stained green with their blood

Chartreuse and red made a person feel dread
Whiskey and wine made a person divine
Water and bread made a person feel fed
Apple and pear made a person beware
A satellite was visible in the middle of the day
Epiphany approached, then skittered away

Daughter removed the headset, she was suggestible enough
For the trial, therefore a quantity of time elapsed
They put sensors on her skin and took them off again
She threw up into a basin shaped like a kidney
They opened a port to administer the therapy
I gave her to them willingly, I waived liability

I was holding the bottoms of her bare feet
They sent her somewhere with a chemical
Hooked into her blood like something placental
Have you ever watched a child develop subjectivity?
Her eyes open slowly, like two dark oars emerging from the mist . . .
Sunlight made a parallelogram on her neck

Circulation meant *blood* but also *money*
Frost tender, a farmer might say, regarding a forageable herb
Over the PA someone said, *Everything's gonna be okay*
A polypropylene doll produced automatic weeping sounds
Over the PA someone said, *If mine eye offend thee, pluck it out*
Daughter had a sunburn in the shape of a parallelogram

—*The ceiling is too close,* said daughter
It's not touching you, I said
—*But the ceiling is touching the air,* said daughter
—*And the air is touching me,* said daughter
—*The air is coming inside me,* said daughter
—*The ceiling is coming inside me,* said daughter

A man stood at the edge of the glacier with a broom
Sweeping water back into the wine-dark sea
Each time he swung his arms forward, a piece of straw
Broke from the broom and sank into the water
Was the environment the container or what it contained
Was the question on no one's mind, we were sick of it

Affordances clung to her like confectioners' sugar
A major adverse event buried the contingency plan
A scoop of bubblegum ice cream melted like unicorn crap
I swiped left in search of a suitably uneventful habitat
And daughter went to school less and less
And daughter was sick and the roads were a mess

People jumped off bridges with cables around their waists
A person lived alone in a cave for four hundred and sixty-four days
Dashboard plastic and molded cupholders cracked in the sun
We covered the paddy field with a big shiny silver blanket
Have you ever watched a child develop shame?
Silence comes over her like the shadow of an alien mothership . . .

To isolate the irritant we isolated the house
To rule out attribution to contagious light or sound
We installed acoustic paneling on daughter's ceiling
And covered her windows with creamy velvet
We gave her soft toys, a hypoallergenic carpet
We generated intimacy by reading each other's diaries

I verified her cycle and we plotted her visions
Daughter lying on her belly, propped up on her elbows
She opened her mouth so I could spoon the liquid in
—A frog swam around and around in a washtub until it drowned
—I was digging a hole, not for any reason, just to dig a hole
It was around that time I started taking the pills

She was making the *bad* sound a wounded bird might make
Splayed like a mammal on the side of the road
When someone has run it over and driven away
She believed that, ultimately, the lucky would die, and
The rest of us would be haunted by the knowledge
Of what we had to do to survive

She wore the sensory dampening suit for the journey
The gallery used to be a bank, old ATMs lined the lobby
There was money on the floor you couldn't spend anymore
Safe inside, far from salient stimuli, I unlatched the visor
That month was a bunch of knockoff Balthus prints
Varnish-brushed so we could pretend they were paintings

Thérèse, her thin red sweater, her Peter Pan collar, all adjectives . . .
She leans back, braced on a single wrist, lovingly rendered
On the hastily sketched bench seat, freeing, like a garrote,
A single thread from her woolen skirt, her white socks
Cuffed below the knee, at ease as a subject, belonging
Utterly to her instant . . .

Anything in a pen was a pig, anything in a frame was a fact
—*You had another daughter before me?* said daughter
I gave her the face that said, *We don't talk about that*
And made my expression harsh in her direction
In a wallpaper-patterned dress daughter was a floating stare
She looked where Thérèse was looking, which was nowhere

I followed daughter with the monitor, dispensing dopamine
Thérèse, that must have been a painful pose for dreaming . . .
She languors and sulks, folds herself forcefully into
The frame to display her ankles, impatient, her asemic elegance
Angled toward, just out of frame, a window, a world
I can only access through the sunlight that touches her face . . .

—*Balthus painted these?* said daughter, reading the wall
Not exactly, the originals were lost; these are only reproductions, I said
—*And your other daughter?* said daughter
On battlefields people said one last thing, then died
—*Am I the reproduction?*
I held the oval between two fingers like a saint

A new hospital was the same place in a different location
The walls of a room reported its inhabitants
Soft and hard surfaces vibrated sympathetically
Boredom sensitized us to overheard speech
Daughter's body was less and less contiguous
We wrapped her in dressings when she dressed

The dog barked at the moon but it wouldn't come down
—*Mama,* said daughter, *What street did the horses live on?*
I don't know, tell me, I said
—*Mane Street!* said daughter, *And why did the horses move?*
I don't know, tell me, I said
—*They didn't like their neeeighborhood!* said daughter

A sentence, like a massacre, had to be answered
Birds in clear-cut woods mimicked heavy machinery
People were tossing buckets of white paint onto the street
To reflect the sunlight, people were planting panic grass
In the medians, between the hulking tractors
People recorded a womb from the inside and played it back

They snapped on the bracelet and put her in solitary
Elsewhere, Elsewhere, I swayed where I stood, sessile as a weed
She lay back on the gurney, shadows clung to her chest
And dripped from her cheekbones like a special effect
I peeled the rinds of my cuticles back and kept going
She coughed into a tissue, black gunk shone there like tar

Daughter was waxy like a memory of someone
You haven't seen in a really, really long time
The screen had twelve faces on it in varying degrees of agony
Twelve faces to communicate the entire range of human feeling
She tapped one in the middle, trying to be brave
I tried not to think about the thirteenth face

It was like she was tuned to every channel at once
Like all her nerve endings were exposed
She glowed like a skinned angel in the bay window
Every leaf of every tree of every wood, went the saying
Her sense of sight had a sense of touch, the world
Penetrated her with detail

The sound of the register was unnervingly similar to a fire alarm
With each purchase the patrons bolted, several were trampled to death
After a few minutes they filed back in as if nothing had happened
It was like the opening and closing of heliotropic flowers, in the lobby
Bodies piled up, blocking out the light and violating several local ordinances
Once an hour or so the shift manager hauled them to the curb

On the grass the dusk just sort of sat there
An old woman walked a red-haired dude on a leash
An old man drove a hay baler from one end of a field to the other
They killed the grasshopper, and she screamed
Over the PA someone said, *Eram quod es, eris quod sum*
Over the PA someone said, *Please, no, not my son*

Daughter spit into the sink, clots curlicued
—*Where does it go?* said daughter
Down through the pipes, I said
—*Then where does it go?* said daughter
Away, for processing, I said
—*When does it stop going away?* said daughter

A flaccid shoot slinked into the ear of a sleeping child
Witnessing a conflict made my otoliths wobble
Sometimes a vehicle swapped a person's components in transit
The whole person is accounted for, the clerk would say
Of course, it was like rearranging all the letters in a book
And insisting it was the same book, all the letters were there

Inky air ached my lungs, it was easier to breathe on the
Floor, hardwood splintered, warmly swelled like a
Newborn, daughter's room, I held her in my arms, watched
Her soul fill her up from the inside, daughter standing on
The street, praise be, daughter's little shadow in the big orange
Light, her eyes strange, like two just-made

Mirrors that hadn't been looked into yet
Smoke poured out of the chimney like an antique postcard of upstate New York in
winter
The dog paced like an ancient entertainer sentenced to exile
My shadow shortened until it fused with me
While the house burned I thought about
What I used to think I'd save if the house were burning

Daughter's pajamas had blue and white stripes with yellow ducks
In the firelight they looked black and yellow with brown ducks
In the firelight a brown duck looked like a rabbit
A rabbit looked like undetached rabbit parts
Coincidentally arranged in a rabbit-like configuration
The slightest change in perspective could shatter the illusion

Creamy, someone wrote, regarding ocean waves
Creamy, someone wrote, regarding the inner arm
Creamy, someone wrote, regarding the attire of musicians
Creamy, someone wrote, regarding trees in Boston
Creamy, someone wrote, regarding a painting of a lemon
Shriveled on the table like a difficult lesson

Irreversible flames dribbled from the open windows
My carefully constructed story for family services
I promised I'd take daughter to a better place
—*The place dead people go?* said daughter
We tried not to squander our trauma
Our descendants would inherit it

I packed her into the back seat just after dinner
Overfed so she'd be too tired to ask questions
And I wouldn't have to hear my falsehoods
Precipitate like a cartoon cumulonimbus between us
At the edge of the regulation football field
I squatted over a drain grate rusted shut

A thick slug of blood slid out of me, then my phone
Slid through the slats and splashed down there
The cracked glass feebly flashed and went dark
Effluvia flew through me unambiguously
—*Mama,* said daughter, I clicked the seat belt in
Daughter, I said, the car smelled like wet grass and urine

The petunias were supreme, daughter put on the goggles
A fruit fly landing on her thigh left a welt
She remembered everything and was tired all the time
Crabgrass bristled at the base of the bluffs
Only the ripples told us we were swimming, at the surface
The sunlight refracted, breaking daughter's leg in half

We squabbled daily over the problem of evil
On mountains people practiced drawing circles
They camouflaged the cameras so you couldn't see them flying
It was around that time I started taking the pills
You could either tumble or run, run or tumble
Or wait forever for permission to be who you are

I dove down and scooped up ageless muck
Sticky and translucent like cervical mucus
Heavy gases pooled at the bottoms of my lungs
Under a circus tent the light was red and gauzy
It was like looking out from the inside of a great
Organ, an organ without a body

We were compelled to adventure like the last prince cut his hair
And rode off on a handsome animal that knew its name
We acknowledged we were observing a flat surface
But relished the illusion of three-dimensional space
As for the trouble, we didn't know how to stay with it
A hero's journey comprised a sequence of pivotal moments

Blobs formed at the brink of my vision, smoothing the edges
People inoculated asylum seekers with patriotic concepts
Over the PA someone asked for help opening a jar of peanut butter
Way up above us hummed billions of wingèd insects
We didn't prepare, we had preparedness plans
Over the PA someone was keeping it light

There were living and nonliving ways of being
Children had bad man practice to rehearse the obligatory song
About what to do if a bad man came, they would have to
Sing it, but quietly, in their heads, that's what the song told to do
I used to sit on the front porch and wave when she got on the bus
She used to bring home drawings of families in basements

Creamy lake, someone wrote, regarding the object of passion
Creamy moons, someone wrote, regarding hothouse chrysanthemums shining
    through the golden gloom
Creamy as a cat, someone wrote, regarding excitement
Creamy iridescent coats of mail, someone wrote, regarding wheelbarrows
Creamy, someone wrote, regarding a beige wall being looked at by someone who
    wasn't anxious
Creamy drops of mammalian weather, someone wrote, regarding the tears of the sun

Daughter wanted to know where the birds went
Daughter wanted to know why the wind burned
Daughter wanted to know what *saudade* meant
Daughter wanted to know if this would be forever
She's right here with me, a mourner might say, putting their palm to their chest
I cut daughter's hair like the last princess

The outskirts of the city were still rendering
Each house on the block was a blurred approximation
With a flat gray façade and half-hearted seasonal decorations
I knelt to film a close-up of a single black ant
Carrying a purple flower across a clump of dry grass
We tried to talk but didn't know what to do with our hands

I once watched a man eat an entire incandescent light bulb
Having watched a man eat a light bulb immediately became information about me
I turned over the newspaper but there was nothing written on the back
Like my predecessors, I suffered from a crisis of character
The man tied the filament in his mouth like a cherry stem
Blood pooled where daughter's teeth met her gums

We built a film set to look like the ruins of an early civilization
The abandoned film set was the ruins of our civilization
Over the PA someone said, *Fetish, implicate, exploit*
A slime mold reached for a cube of granulated sugar
My passport was so *good* I didn't think of it as good
My passport was so *good* I didn't think of it at all

It was difficult to speak honestly
Because it was difficult to think honestly
As for the islands of trash in the middle of the oceans
Sometimes I thought about them, then I thought about the next thing
Because it was difficult to speak honestly
It was difficult to think, honestly

The medicine made her head sunflower-heavy
Inside my passport was a picture of a bear eating a fish
Inside my passport was a picture of a bald eagle and a buffalo
The caption said, *Is our world gone? We say "Farewell"*
Is a new world coming? We welcome it—
And we will bend it to the hopes of man

I strapped daughter in and we got going
Bugs made abstract expressions on the windshield
Scientists put jellyfish genes in a rabbit
The g-forces were delectable in my pelvis
We had retained the word *mammoth* to talk about big things
A mammoth was a big animal that used to exist

Her eardrums ached so I closed the window
People awaited rations in neat rows like beech trees in a plantation forest
The parallax made her dizzy so I turned off her eyes
On an intercity bus a person decapitated another person
An atrocity was news, then memory, then history, then myth
In the soundproof dungeon, the sound of a whip

People carved baroque monuments out of Styrofoam
And spray-painted them gold and left them outside mansions
On immaculate lawns with alarmed sprinklers
It was a joke, a joke about money, and who had it
And who did not, and who would suffer and who would not
And whose inklings leaked out inconveniently, leaving viscous, odoriferous trails . . .

At the edge of her skin there were cells and hairs and heat
Continents smashed and made mountains ascend
A man opening his trench coat had something for sale
Apprehension meant *knowledge* but also *dread*
Whoever had the remedy could hold the world hostage
Inside of understanding, a creamy center of fear

A horse's nostrils flared over my swollen knuckles
Another new extinction, another new therapy
I couldn't tell if a cave was a cave or a replica cave from a natural history museum
I couldn't tell if a cloud was a supercell or a forest fire
I couldn't tell if a cemetery was a cemetery
Or a shop that used to sell tombstones

The road went on forever and was very straight
The economic metaphor gave way to the ecological metaphor
I put the oval between my teeth and my gums
My body retaliated in an electrochemical manner
People pulled over on the shoulder practiced photosynthesizing
We smeared cyanobacteria on the backs of our necks

My hands shook as I filmed her shaking in the wind
Inside her, I thought, there must be another wind
I got an occurrence for looking at the sky wrong
Daughter dissembled, disassembled daughter
I stood on a dune and classified her prodromes
Deploying the *good* news slowly so it wouldn't run out

The guy behind the camera asked kids to speak in tongues
Primitivity scored high on metrics across the sector
Pollen interfaced with the blood-brain barrier
I pulled down my mask to draw on some credit
R stood for Romeo, *H* stood for Hotel
Teenagers perched on a granite outcropping howled

—*I want to go back,* said daughter
Home? Do you miss your things? I said
—*I want to go back to before I was born,* said daughter
Bummer, a mother might say, regarding birth
Animacies crawled over us, we grimaced away
We can get you new things, I said

Barely is how the vehicle moved through the quarantine zone
People paused in the designated place to pose for a photograph
With an open-mouthed mountain lion someone had just killed
Signals broadcast up and down my peripherals
Peach pits in landfills sent shoots down into the rot
A pain was like a sound, you couldn't turn it off

Daughter bobbed like a buoy in the rearview mirror
She was everywhere, or starting to be everywhere
Our clothing no longer suggested a life unburdened by worry
We kept waiting for an emergency to announce itself
There was no inciting incident, there were only *situations*
Over the PA someone said, *Powerless, but not helpless*

In camps along the highway we transformed our thoughts
Looking at screens made me think in screens
Had I remembered to regularize the account books?
I turned on the wipers and the defroster, I could hear her
Rustling in the back seat as we passed the dump
Her breath smelled ominous, like bad oil

A roadside weed could scratch you as you passed it
The lesion greened until cell walls repeated
In your bloodstream and your body went turgid
Like a leaf, from the extremities in, until only
Your heartbeat remained and your lungs going up
And down like a vulture in a thermal column

Droplets condensed inside us as we slept
A mother's intact gaze coerced her offspring
With her head in a tree hole daughter told her secrets
Nature turned into culture and then back again
Have you ever watched a child develop sacrifice?
Calm comes over her like a memory of ice-skating in an indoor rink in the middle
of summer . . .

Bruises on our hips turned brown or purple or yellow
I put her feet in the sleeping bag, pulled it up like a cocoon
How I love my babe-a-la, little baby girl, I sang
How I love my sweet-a-la, little baby girl, I sang
How I love my only, little baby pony, I sang
How I love your fat and fur, little baby daughter, I sang

In a subjunctive mood I met a horse, he was one big warm muscle under the palm
of my hand
He looked at me the way people looked at each other in convenience stores
Before the *situation,* trying to recognize each other out of context
When I touched him, the word *libido* flew into me like a sparrow
Into a window, we used to put a decal of a hawk on the glass
To teach the songbirds architecture

I added another log and the fire grew up
—*Is it alive?* said daughter
No, but it will go out without wood and air, I said
—*How does it know where the air is?* said daughter
It doesn't know anything, I said
We unrolled the tarp and inspected it

One man was trying to decide whether or not to keep
An album of photographs of his little boy
Smiling with a helmet, sepia in the firelight
The man kicked embers into the pit and sighed
A filament of spittle stretched between his lips
He watched the fire, I watched the flames in his glasses

Fugitive, a scholar might say, regarding knowledge
The face of my watch was disfigured, I couldn't tell
The time, locusts chewed holes through my lexicon
Daughter wanted to know what the pills were
Daughter wanted to know how the gun worked
Elsewhere, said the billboard on the side of the highway

At the edge of one town a boy pressed one end of his flute
Into an anthill and started to play a melody I could not hear
The ants were large and red and biting him on his wrists and ankles
And the tops of his bare feet, leaving angry red injuries
A few people egged him on, the rest of us cried
And begged him to stop, he didn't

The supermarket was iffy, we tied the dog to a post
Are you ever going to name that thing? I asked daughter
—*I love her,* said daughter
How do you know she loves you? I asked daughter
The dog was stained and crumpled like the butt of a cigarette
—*I know she could kill me, and she chooses not to,* said daughter

Ripe bananas just sat there like they weren't even scarce
People memorized monologues and amused each other
People ate Iranian pistachios in a library courtyard
Behind a fence a horse was furred and dark and so specific
When I looked at it, I felt something like dedication
No—devotion . . .

Looking at pixels made me think in pixels
I chewed the oval in the middle of the cereal aisle
Never show an idiot a half-finished job, went the saying
Our eyes were staring, our mouths were open, our wings were spread
With the wreckage of history on our wretched heads
She's gone, a mother might say, regarding the dog

Someone in yellow harvested corneas from the killing field
When you touched something, it touched you back, I read that once
Then I thought about that for twelve years without thinking about anything else
A person went for a drive, betrayed their deeply held principles
It was better to be patient zero than patient one
We denatured game in the sun

The car made a sound like an air-raid siren, I ran the wipers
A crescent moon could cut into you like a sickle
Dozens of fossils rained down onto the hood
They made a sound like grains of rice falling on a cymbal
We foraged for beneficial compounds in half-built beachfront condos
Like two apostles, we lay in the tent with our foreheads pressed together, daughter
and I

Legal death was when a person could no longer
Engage in commerce with the outside world
I couldn't tell if a constellation was made of stars or satellites
I couldn't tell if a star was a star or a planet
I couldn't tell if a planet was inhabitable or not
The treatment blued daughter like a distant mountain

A wolf scooped ice into its mouth to hide its breath
Someone spilled hot coffee down the front of their shirt
I reached inside the horse to exteriorize the heart
And hung it upside down like a fistful of wildflowers
She sat patiently in the back seat drawing horses
Over the PA someone told an origin story

What had happened could happen and therefore felt inevitable
A man jumping off a bridge thought, *I have made a terrible mistake*
The purpose of the rain was to be small and wet
The purpose of a flower was to be obeyed
A dehumanized person couldn't be rehumanized again
It was like trying to manicure a hedge into the shape of a hedge

Pieces of plastic collected in the bellies of freshwater fish
Indiscriminate trawlers hauled creatures into their cavities
To preserve a dying tradition required a sterile jam jar
If you said *mane,* I would think of the horse
If you said *humane,* I would think of destroying him
We learned to drink milk by mimicking calves

People stood in plazas with clipboards and vests
In cleanrooms people milked horseshoe crabs of their blood
The memory of a kiss outlasted the kiss
Does critique belong to the object or only refer to it
Was the question on no one's mind, we longed for the sensation of a thumbnail
Slid pleasurably into shrink-wrap

In one town the streets were lined with identical white houses
One had a whole shelf of *To the Lighthouse*
Each edition with a different painting on the cover
Impressionist, pointillist, cubist, nothing abstract
And each painting unmistakably of a lighthouse
At night there were horrible screams from the sealed garages

Eyeless and terrible, said the book, and the book was right
Pain was the shadow of a bird on the shadow of a branch
Daughter bucked like a fledgling in the back seat
An unprovoked act of senseless brutality was hardly mentioned
We passed from territory to adventure and back again
That's the whole point, one might say, regarding it

People felt touchy re: metaphors about alienation
People took turns influencing each other
The medium is the message, went the saying
Daughter's boots made a sound like chewing gravel
A raven ought to have learned to love a scarecrow
The way a child learns to love neglect

Creamy with tenderness, someone wrote, regarding a child's affections
Creamy pulp, someone wrote, regarding a brain cut by a scalpel
Creamy, someone wrote, regarding a sumptuous evening
Creamy, someone wrote, regarding a flower's waxen flesh
Creamy, someone wrote, regarding a brook full of garbage
We didn't know what to do with our garbage

Clouds fast-forwarded over a high-contrast skyline
Flowers grew and bloomed and died and that was time passing
Canines alerted at the stink of two people embracing each other
And jawed them apart, as they had been trained to do
The way a ball python encircles a deer mouse, or the sea penetrates a paper cup
when the paper cup has blown, unnoticed, into the sea
That was how our circumstances were immersed in us

People fell asleep with their noses in each other's armpits
People tossed a tennis ball from their left hand to their right
People cleared their throats and excused themselves
People summarized an interaction in order to signal its conclusion
People kept a shoebox full of sentimental shit
People tried to make it look like they were just going on a trip

People unbuttoned their jackets to indicate the desire to sit
People hiding under cafeteria tables got shot in the high school
People on skateboards leaned in the direction they wanted to turn
People drinking slushies got shot in the food court
People learning to write their names got shot in the elementary school
People got shot watching the parade with their families

People untied the belts from their arms and leaned back
People talking to God got shot in the synagogue
People in child's pose got shot at a yoga studio
People depositing paychecks got shot in banks
People made their own soap to sell at the local farmers market
People buying eggs got shot at the grocery store

People slid the specimen into the tray and sanitized their hands
People riding the subway got shot coming home from the park
People formed intimate bonds with inanimate objects
People hiding in bathroom stalls got shot in nightclubs
I thought it was firecrackers, said the DJ
People holding signs got shot at peaceful protests

People drinking soda got shot in a bowling alley
People hiding behind racks of blue T-shirts got shot in department stores
People hiding behind heavy-duty printers got shot in offices
People practiced saying vowels while a therapist touched their mouth
People put their hands around each other's throats and had orgasms
People marked the box that said they would give away their organs

The sky turned mauve, I turned on the headlights
Something shone on the vanishing point, something bright
Came closer and closer until finally we were upon him—
Grazing the dense mists, his back hunched like a desert
Ridge in a watercolor painting, when the dust settles
Over the setting sun, holy is the color of the foothills—

He was on fire, the horse—
A fire that burned with no smoke, it started at the mane
And trailed down his lips, a muzzle of fire, ashes swirled
Around his nostrils, a fire that spread its tendrils where he grazed
On the roadside, the way the twilight should spread
Over a forest floor under a crown-shy canopy, *dappled*—

On his face there were black flies—hundreds
They were massed around the horse's eyes—hundreds
They were drinking the horse's tears—hundreds
The sound was like a hundred downed power lines
Dipping into a hundred frozen ponds
Daughter used the black crayon in the back seat

It smelled like acetone and sulfur
His tail burned like a special occasion
His hooves charred and cracked, he rolled his eyes
In protest, then bent his head to the grass
Daughter met the horse's gaze as we passed
And held it until the fire went out

Over the PA someone said, *Expect miracles!*
And the rest, as they say, is history, went the saying
There were antediluvian arks, prelapsarian fruits
The record was oral, then archive, then digital, then moot
Pain was still painful even after the source of the pain was removed
We wrote our love letters in the present tense

We congregated on foot in the strip mall parking lot
Over the PA someone said, *Be the change!*
Headlights shone, as watchful as wolves' eyes
Someone's tires had flattened a crow onto the asphalt
One wing flapped free from the matted mass
Like a flag at half-mast

Elsewhere, said the decal on the side of the van
A man in a white uniform took our temperatures
He had a name tag that said *Hank* with three foil stars on it
And, in smaller letters, the words *I Believe It!*™
We filled out paperwork, he buckled daughter in first
Beside a boy in a blue and white sailor-stripe shirt

Some people were born who couldn't feel damage
They were the most vulnerable and had to be protected
An unsuccessful launch sparkled like a meteor
My thoughts were organized by an intelligence I didn't recognize
Hank told me to leave my possessions behind
And handed me a badge with a name that wasn't mine

I babbled like a baby in the center of the Sharing Circle
There were lost maps and failures of organization
There were glass deserts and people dead from radiation
They changed the name of the place we came from
And reminded us how badly we had been treated there
And noted our disclosures in a leather-bound book

I ate from the apple, and the apple tree cried out
Hank pointed to the way I wrote the letter *A*
I didn't want to be a conduit for anything
When the blindfold came off, I still couldn't see
For one eternity I thought they had blinded me
Dark is how it was on the inside of my body

I heard laughter and then an electric hum, around me
Four thick glass walls pressed—a disused aquarium, maybe
There were lights all around me, I was dripping, I was clothed
But felt naked like a child reading complex and disturbing
Verse they can't comprehend to an imaginary audience
Hank sat with his arms folded in a row of seated people

I started to hear a faint tapping, tap tap tap tap
We are the keepers of history, said the man in the pony mask
At first I guarded the light jealously, like a dragon guards gold
I searched the masked faces but none of them were daughter's
Beetles were scuttling along the walls, tap tap tap tap
I felt the intervention, suddenly, I was so . . . lonely . . .

Moths were gathering against the walls, tap tap tap tap
I wanted to be drawn, I wanted to press myself
To the sun and leave my silhouette there, smoldering . . .
I'll see it when I Believe It!™ said the man in the pony mask
Fireflies were beating against the walls, tap tap tap tap
I wanted to tear up my life and give it away . . .

Looking at reflections made me think in reflections
Selfhood is parasitic, said the man in the pony mask
I tried to focus on the sounds of the moths, their soft bodies
Rustled like paperbacks, I read every wing, electrified
Heat trickled from between my legs, sliding
In and out of me, nitrogen and oxygen vibrating . . .

The chamber shook, cracks were forming
In the glass, the shadows of the moths upon me
Inside me, tap tap tap tap, remaking me entirely
I was *dappled*—forgiven—finally free
I closed my eyes, they wrapped me in *good* leaves
That was how we joined the community

My perspective did not adequately integrate
Therefore they induced me and took the *bad* parts out
Elsewhere, Elsewhere, I wanted to be with daughter
Elsewhere, Elsewhere, I wanted to be like daughter
The deer dreaded the leopard but never wanted leopards to not exist
As for prosperity, we didn't know what to do with it

The sound of an empty was the opposite of a rattle
Hank made construction-paper snowflakes with a box cutter
I could not remember not being a mother
When daughters were born here, they cut them in half
Delicate new daughters sprang from the parts pruned back
New delicacies

She encountered the spiked rampion
She squeezed dew out of the maiden's-tears
She withstood the blue mallow, the arrow broom was a portent
The vetch met her eyeball-to-eyeball, she stumbled upon a coronilla
The false baby's breath accommodated, blessed milk-thistle opined
She read the words, but they didn't form a picture in her mind

The community was a type of assistive technology, like a spiderweb
                              a type of physical memory, like a spiderweb
                              a type of information processor, like a spiderweb
                              a type of reciprocal causation, like a spiderweb
                              a type of extended cognition, like a spiderweb
The community pulled taut conveyed the subtlest vibrations

The brain surveilled the body, the body multiplied in secret
We witnessed our thoughts, they were not ours
Little black feathers fell out of the sky like commas
A thought was simply an occurrence, like a fly landing on an apple core browning in the sun was an occurrence, or track lights flickering in a foyer was an occurrence, or newspapers accumulating at the bottom of an old man's driveway
Daughter and I pressed our respirators together
Like we used to kiss goodnight

Elsewhere, said the sign welded to the big iron gates
Daughter had no depth, but she could dilate
On the border wall was freshly tagged
I don't wanna have to kill myself
I breathed in and out, polluting my surroundings
Little blue buildings in a big green valley

An experiment with the past demanded replication
We baked bread, killing some other organisms
A balcony once made you choose between freedom and privacy
A credit card once made you choose between freedom and privacy
A lover once made you choose between freedom and privacy
We washed our hands, killing some other organisms

As for privacy, we didn't know what to do with it
When I lie to the community, I lie to myself, went the saying
The conditioned stimulus was a philodendron in a terra-cotta pot
Daughter swung a cardboard sword in the recreation area
Daughter transcribed the teachings onto a scroll
Fear extinction followed nonreinforced exposure

The *situation* was processed for evidentiary purposes
And objects from the scene gathered for later prosecution
There was no phonological loop, no visuospatial sketch pad
When I lie to the community, said the man in the pony mask
I lie to myself, we all said back
I put the oval in the palm of my hand

Onto the dusk-charged air we welded a new preposition
A bottom-feeding fish wasn't sure how to interact with its reflection
Empty like an airport terminal, an emptiness that lubricates fantasy . . .
The acquisition window slid shut and I was feral forever
Spontaneous discourse combusted in the crowd
Dragonflies blinked

Daughter on her back, talking to the daddy longlegs
Cycling her feet in the air, her toenails painted lime green
She had a scrunchie around her ankle with a silk begonia on it
A pigeon participated in a token economy
Its cheeks got fat in the wall of cages
Even the thinnest threshold took up space

Time moved swiftly inside the community
We romanticized a former era we perceived as more authentic
It was hard to remember what exactly a dollar looked like
We cherished our purity and narrowed our trust
Could have, ought to have, might have, will
It was around that time I started taking the pills

Mornings we stood in the Sharing Circle
I deserve my success, we said, one at a time, counterclockwise
The words were like glass pebbles my mouth polished
The word *wildlife* sounded exotic and almost plausible
Over the PA someone subtitled the world, after an hour
We'd gone five or six rounds and I deserved my success

I knew I should feel outraged but I didn't know why
If you couldn't create, you could just plagiarize, it was impossible
To tell the difference, a person's eyes didn't really light up
When they had an idea in their head, not like in the novels
Besides, we were not making discoveries so much
As learning what we already knew

I dreamt of daughter on the beach, it was winter
The beautiful hands of synchronized swimmers were going up and down in the water
Surf sparkled in the sun like stallions showing off
Dress shirt sleeves on the sand had arms in them
Over the PA someone said, *You don't really care for music, do ya?*
I woke up and realized those were people drowning

Daughter was bent over her notebook, it said *HORSE*
What's that you're writing? I asked
—I'm not writing, she said, *I'm drawing*
—It's a drawing of a HORSE
With her index finger she traced the edge of the page
—It's a drawing of a HORSE in a cage

Daughter in the garden, caressing the grass
Creamy, someone wrote, regarding a woman in a dress
Creamy, the sharpened edge of a ceramic knife
Creamy, a stone, limestone
On the anterior banister a bug waved one thingy around
Over the PA someone said, *You know your mother doesn't like to be disturbed when she's watching the war*

The space between *good* and *bad* began to diminish
Daughter studied botany while I analyzed the transference
Over the PA someone said, *And the wisdom to know the difference*
We integrated our sensory impressions into a coherent scene
Her hair was getting long, her eyes were turning green
As for wisdom, we didn't know what to do with it

There was a time before and after thinking of death
As the worst thing that could happen to a person
Bodies were interred and then exhumed again
Satisfactory, said Hank, which meant the opposite
We had overestimated our capacity for wonder
We had underestimated our capacity for pain

Quiver, quaver, flutter, squirm, twitch
Shimmy, wobble, shake, convulse, twist
Tremble, jerk, shudder, vibrate, writhe
Jiggle, bobble, sway, waggle, die
Remedial media rehabilitated me as needed
Daughter's doll had real lashes and handmade clothes

Daughter stood in front of the tank, bathed in green light
On the screens I could watch her from every angle
Her outline was woolly, it was like trying to see through
A blizzard, hypotheticals swirled up around her feet
A green limb rose from the liquid, when it broke the surface
She looked surprised, like a bystander who's just been hit

Then she was extending herself toward it, groping
The green shallows, aimlessly, as though she couldn't see
Her outline indiscriminate, her outline arbitrary
It wrapped around her waist and pulled her under
Inside my passport there were stamps from other places, places I had been
On purpose, on creamy blue paper, I hated her

The oxygenation of the Earth was a catastrophe, said the man in the pony mask
The oxygenation of the Earth was a genocide, we all said back
A shaded sapling borrowed sugar from its friends
Our bodies remembered pathogens we had encountered before
Our bilateral symmetry gave us crude confidence
We liked the taste of fats and sugars most of all

She came up gasping, but they wouldn't let me in
Tell me what you feel, daughter, said the man in the pony mask
She's not your daughter, I said
She's not my daughter, said the man in the pony mask
She's my daughter, I said
She's not your daughter, said the man in the pony mask

There were tallgrass, midgrass, and shortgrass regions
Foragers, scavengers, predators, prey
Exhibiting behaviors, we sometimes said, like the soul was a gallery wall
On which the shadow of a stand of bamboo was cast by a passing headlight
In the middle of the night, when the canvases can finally look at each other
Truthfully, regarded and regarding, together and alone, the way a man rests his hand on his thigh while he waits in the haze for the ferry that will take him, finally, to the other side

Evenings we looked at pictures and talked about what they meant
Daughter, thinly distributed like a colony of aphids
She spoke half a sentence and then she was spent
Root hairs pivoted on the dirt like legs of centipedes
She had learned how to make seeds germinate instantly
As for grief, I was terrified by the seclusion of it

There was promise, she said, in the lichen
A plastic bag blew around in the visible spectrum
Color participated in our interpretation of the seasons
Rain is only rain in midair, went the saying
It was around that time I started taking the pills
We quenched the plants so they wouldn't erupt

Daughter in a daze, disseminating herself
The sunset glared in every window in the community
We watched all five hundred and thirty-four sunsets
Her name tag had eight foil stars on it, more than any of us
She reached into heartwood, gummed with an ingredient
Testing the seepage between her thumb and forefinger

Daughter chewed the end of a pencil from surplus
—*What's an ontological sickness?* said daughter
Who taught you that word? I said
She looked at Hank without moving her face
When I looked at her, I felt something like degraded
No—jilted . . .

Indefinite postponement, said Hank
This meant we would never be acquitted
Pipelines spilled like entrails from a half-eaten lamb
Hank pressed a foil star onto my name tag
—*I don't have access; I am access*, said daughter
As for the wind, the smoke told me what I needed to know

At night I folded her uniforms into rectangles
Ask and ye shall believe, went the saying
Hank surveilled us for symptoms of treason
I worked in the garden harvesting solid volumes
Daughter was, I understood, a kind of hazard
She threatened to assimilate the entire world

Everyone in the Sharing Circle was flapping their arms
Meals arrived on trays, we inserted them into our tracts
—*Am I really your daughter?* said daughter
Her back arched like a person that had just begun to be hit by a car
Of course you are, I said
—*Like your arm is your arm?* said daughter

My mask had two vertical slits for eyeholes
I squinted out of it like a medieval archer
Daughter's mask was a translucent sphere
Only the glare told me she was wearing it
A maid stood next to a window pouring milk
People looked at her and wondered what she was thinking

A drawing had hesitation marks where someone wasn't sure
A wrist had hesitation wounds where someone wasn't sure
Like my predecessors, I suffered from a crisis of nostalgia
We observed patterns, tones, lines, and colors
Meanwhile daughter was more and more ambient
A sheet hung up to dry twisted like a ghost in the wind

Have you ever watched a child develop sex?
Death comes over her like a skyscraper blotting out the sun . . .
Daughter dreaming with her face toward the core
Turned slowly in her sleep like a fragile planet
Over the PA someone said, *Nor again is there anyone who loves or pursues or desires*
To obtain pain of itself, because it is pain

Over the PA someone said, *Close down the gallery*
The surgeons began by inflicting a wound
And aimed a bright light into her darkness
Over the PA someone said, *Retractor, please*
I waited in cold blood in the room we used for meetings
They fed us vanilla cupcakes with chocolate frosting

Elsewhere, we were living to completion
A spoken word is not a sparrow, went the saying
The sutures would heal over, leaving barely a scar
Where the old reality had been, like a long-forgotten fever
To each his own purpose? said the man in the pony mask
I Believe It!™ we all said back

You could put tears on a slide and examine them for a reason
You could breathe headfirst in the ice at the base of a pine
You could refuse all ideology, which was an ideology
We attended to the climate the way a fly
Attends to the spider in whose web it's caught
A father taught his son where to put his apologies

A single encounter could contaminate you for life
People wanted to watch videos of people struggling
E.g., a boy pretending to catch and then eat a salmon
Another boy comes along and steals the salmon, etc.
The surgeons pulled at the flap like a little door
An actor held their breath to be dead

The image was not available in my territory
I sat in the ward for hours but couldn't imagine anything
All speech was a form of advertisement
All observation was a form of confession
To reveal the wires, they opened daughter's wrists
There were only vines

What quality of life was worth preserving?
The dominant metaphor for thought was virality
An idea was something to which one might be "exposed"
And realigned in an instant like shocked quartz
The hierarchy of sentience was tacitly unimpeachable
Under the asphalt, the treacherous goo

On the cliff people stopped talking about the cliff
That was the funny thing about the cliff
One by one we watched the bodies dangle and fall
When a body survived, that was a miracle
When a miracle survived, it became an individual
But an individual could not survive

What would happen to me would not hurt, I felt sure
What hurt was to know exactly what would happen
I followed the crowd back to the cliff
And joyously, rapturously, I jostled for my turn
And when the valley was full before I could jump
Guilt curled through me, curdled through me

There were other valleys, to be sure, other daughters
I could recognize but couldn't recollect
Subjunctive moods, birthday parties, the future perfect
Happiness is a choice, said the man in the pony mask
Fate sat on your knee like a child and told you what it wanted
As for wanting, we didn't know what to do with it

Capacious horse, ludicrous horse, undulant horse
You could drive to the dollar store and buy a packet
Of butternut squash seeds, they weren't even proprietary
My brain generated opinions in response to things, it had nothing to do with me
As for agency, half the bullets were spent
There were no causes anymore, there were only origins

In the morning I wrung out my dreams into a basin
Swirled like oil slicks in a gas station parking lot puddle
I wiped the ointment onto daughter's back
Moving my hands in a figure eight
I washed dishes below a running faucet
And the water went away

She walked into the meadow, I watched her through the window
And I watched her name the buttercups' yellows
At the core of the planet a terrible fire burned
She cowered in the grass, she lipped the pistils
The scent of growth was the scent of decay
On the planet's surface her slender fingers clawed the clay

Their sharp and shiny leaves were slim as wrists
She ran her tongue along the stamen to the tip
A stem bent gently and slid inside, thin and thornless
The blossom made her water, she winked and dripped
Sky covered Earth like a poultice
Petals licked at her like flames exchanging softnesses

Daughter arched her back, the roots wrapped her fists
Like vines on the pillars of oracles' temples
As a ripple inflects a pond
As two clouds become one
As blood in the milk makes the calf cry
As a spider's silk tautens to taste the fly

Two butterflies flitted in her folds
A smear of pollen stained her gold, she writhed
Like dew comes on the grass, rain came on the lake
Lorem ipsum dolor in the shade
She wrapped her fists in roots, she flowered in its mouth
She sighed, she wilted, she lay down

AUTHOR'S NOTE

Vexations is titled and structured after Erik Satie's solo piano composition of the same name.

Voices other than "mine" can be heard throughout the poem. For further reading, I particularly recommend Anna Tsing's *The Mushroom at the End of the World: On the Possibility of Life in Capitalist Ruins* (Princeton, NJ: Princeton University Press, 2015), Emanuele Coccia's *The Life of Plants: A Metaphysics of Mixture* (Cambridge: Polity Press, 2019), and Sylvia Fein's *Heidi's Horse* (Pleasant Hill, CA: Exelrod Press, 1984).

Satie's performance instructions read "Très lent" (Very slow) and "Pour se jouer 840 fois de suite ce motif, il sera bon de se préparer au préalable, et dans le plus grand silence, par des immobilités sérieuses." (To play this motif to yourself 840 times in succession, it would be good to prepare yourself beforehand, and in the greatest silence, by serious immobilities.)

I first heard Satie's *Vexations* performed by a procession of pianists—from dawn to dawn, twenty-four hours straight—in "the gallery next to the cafeteria" at the California State Summer School for the Arts (CSSSA) on the campus of CalArts. I was sixteen. That experience planted the seed for this poem, which is also a text score designed to accompany Satie's music.

Thank you to the team at the Fondation Jan Michalski in Montricher, Switzerland, where I composed much of *Vexations* as a resident artist in the summer of 2019.

Thank you to the University of Texas at Austin, the selection committee for the Keene Prize, and my mentors at the James A. Michener Center for Writers. I am particularly grateful to Lisa Olstein (whose reading of John Ashbery gave me the courage to continue pursuing this project), Bret Anthony Johnston, Joanna Klink, and Roger Reeves. Thank you to my teachers, past and present.

Thank you to the friends and family who have helped usher *Vexations* into being in some form, including Auden Lincoln-Vogel, Melissa Lewis, Natasha Barnes, Rose Lewis, Juliet Shafto, Arianna Rebolini, Eleanor Eli Moss, Ryan Paradiso, Raye Hendrix, Jason Grier, Hedgie Choi, Ale Kolleeny, Jeff Koren, Gaia Rajan, Elisa Wouk Almino, and Frida and Stuart Swerdloff.

Thank you to K. Verlag and to Etienne Turpin, Faye Campbell, and Anna-Sophie Springer. Thank you to the University of Chicago Press and to the editors of the Phoenix Poets series, who have so generously welcomed *Vexations*.

Annelyse Gelman